RACING
HUMMINGBIRDS

JULIAN —
HONOR DOESN'T TOUCH
IT. I'M YET PERIOD
THE POEMS PERIOD.
Jean

BY JEANANN VERLEE

A Write Bloody Book
Long Beach. CA USA

Racing Hummingbirds
by Jeanann Verlee

Write Bloody Publishing ©2010.
1st printing.
Printed in USA

Published by Write Bloody Publishing.

Printed in Long Beach, CA USA.

Cover Designed by Joshua Grieve
Cover Art by Tyson Schroeder
Interior Layout by Lea C. Deschenes
Edited by Roger Bonair-Agard, Jon Sands, Adam Falkner, Derrick Brown
Proofread by Sarah Kay, Taylor Mali
Type set in Helvetica Neue and Bell MT

To contact the author, send an email to writebloody@gmail.com

WRITE BLOODY PUBLISHING
LONG BEACH, CA

*for my father
who is not unlike the moon*

THANK YOU

Jon Sands • Roger Bonair-Agard • Cristin O'Keefe Aptowicz • Adam Falkner
Without you, this book would not be. My thanks to you is infinite.

With extended and incomparable thanks to:
Eboni Hogan, Christine Hatch, J.W. Basilo, Adam Bowser, Derrick
Brown and the entire Write Bloody Family, Tyson Schroeder, Sarah
Kay, Taylor Mali, Patricia Smith, Ross Gay, Rachel McKibbens, Marty
McConnell, David Ayllon, Tristan Silverman, Mahogany Browne,
Shappy Seasholtz, Chad Anderson, Nicole Homer, Jared Singer, Darian
Dauchan, Rico Frederick, Akua Doku, Jamie Kilstein, Lynne Procope,
Oveous Salcedo, Jeff Kay, Ed Menchavez, Daemond Arrindell, Anis
Mojgani, Brian S. Ellis, Mike McGee, Karen Finneyfrock, Scott Beal, Les
Lopes, Richard Loranger, Sarena Straus, Randy Thomas, Dr. Marilyn
A. Hetzel, Sandra M. Doe, Jessi Robertson, Wess "Mongo" Jolley, The
Urbana Poetry Slam Family, The louderARTS Project, The LoserSlam
Family, The Nuyorican Family, The SWAP 2008 Family, and Bowery
Poetry Club

And my family, both blood and borrowed, who never let me stop:
Scott and Linda Harris, Judy Davies and Michael Carroll, Brian Bean,
Rhonda Harris, The Harrises, The Ayerses, Dennis Greeley, Jon Deal,
Julie Houston, Missy Wahlers, Jenn Stewart, Melissa Brides, LoMa
Familar, Ronnie Raley, James Barlow, Ben Rollman, Michael Fitzgerald,
Russell Steward, Gregg Mockenhaupt, Amber McFarland, Phillip
Gaskin, Elly Ney Knight-Braun, Karen Bellavia, The Familars, The
Fitzgeralds, and The Greeleys

And my always girl:
Callisto

And finally:
You

RACING HUMMINGBIRDS

LULLABY

COMMUNION

I know a boy who called his girlfriend's body a "crime scene." Dad, my body *is* a crime scene. My body is lint and gasoline and matchstick. My body is a brush fire. It's ticking, Dad, a slow alarm. I have rain boots. Lots of them. It isn't raining anymore. The words are coming back, Dad. The way they fit and jump in the mouth. I want ice cream and long letters. I want to read long love letters but I don't think he loves me. I think I'm used up. I think I'm the grit under his nails, the girl who looks good in pictures. I don't think he loves me. I think they broke me, Dad. I think I drink too much and it's because they broke me. I heard about two girls recently, two women crushed like cherries in a boy's jaw. It opened me, Dad. My body is melted wax, it is ripe and stink and bent. It is a mistake. I walk like an apology. I don't hate men, Dad, I don't. I want a washing machine. I want someone else to do the dishes, someone to walk the dog. I have a hornet in my head, Dad. A hornet. She's an angry bitch. She hurls herself against my skull. She stings. And stings. I know I don't make sense, Dad. This is the problem. I'm a sick girl, a crazy wishbone. I have razors under my tongue. I'm sorry I cut you, Dad, I'm so—*so* sorry. I gave you a card for Father's Day once, it said you were my hero. You are. Your laugh is a thunderclap, you love like surgery. I think they broke me, Dad. I can't erase their faces. I want to swim, Dad. Remember when I used to hopscotch? I used to make you laugh. My feet are hot. The bottoms of my feet are scorched sand, August asphalt. My body is a slug, a mob of sticky wet rot. No one touches me anymore because I'm rot. Because my body is a spill no one wants to clean up. They cracked me open, Dad, I know you don't want to hear about it. You don't want to hear how they scissored me, how they gnawed me like raw meat. No one wants to hear how they made me drink lemon juice, how they kicked the dog, how they upturned the furniture, no one wants to hear how my skin turned to a dark thick of purple and black and lead. I watch the homeless a lot, Dad. I watched a man with a cup of coins and chips of skin carved out of his face. He had freckles. He needs medicine, Dad. He

15

needs to stop the hornet. My body is a hive. I am red ants and jellyfish. A yellow sickness. My body is a used condom in an alley in Jersey City. I don't think he loves me, Dad. My body is a fetus in a biohazard tank. A Polaroid pinned to a corkboard in Brooklyn. I think I'm hurt, Dad. I think I was the tough girl for too long. My body is a wafer, a thin, soft melt on a choir boy's tongue.

THE TELLING

She is a tornado.
He is a man. He is solid and humble.
She tells the story three times, convinced
he does not understand. He is trying.
The story is about an elephant and a mermaid.
No, the story is about a millipede in a thicket of roses,
a prized buckskin horse and fifty lashes.
She is talking gibberish. He is trying to understand but she
is thunderbolt. Her tongue, a spear.
The dog is hiding in the back corner of a dark room.
The man wants to sit with the dog. She is melting.
Her face pools in her lap. Freckles pile at her feet.
There is nothing in the room that has not been hurled.
She is science like this. An atom, separating.
Finally, the story comes, like flood. Its mud seeps in
from under the doorjambs, rising. They are standing
ankle deep in water and sludge. He understands now.
He is a spiced wound. He wants firearms. Hit-men. A brutal justice.
All the while, the window is sitting with its mouth open,
spilling their hot storm into the courtyard,
where the neighbors have come to their sills,
elbows propped, hungry
like vultures.

40 LOVE LETTERS

Dear Dennis,
I still think of you.

Dear Andre,
I saw you kiss her.
I haven't looked back.

Dear Patrick,
You're just too young.

Dear Eric,
I said horrible things about you.
Your teeth are fine,
it's the rest of you I don't like.

Dear Greg,
Thank you for the poem, for every single scar.

Dear William,
I love you, simple.
I like that we will never be *we*.

Dear Jay,
The bruises fell off eventually.

Dear Michael,
I'll never be enough to fill the shoes
that will one day stand at your side.

Dear Ben,
I did read your letters.
All of them.

Dear Freeman,
I'll never stop looking over my shoulder,
boots laced, ready to run.

Dear Jon,
I'll always love you.
You are all there ever was.

Dear Derek,
There was no one thing,
your everything is impossible.

Dear Eddie,
We are refracting magnets.
We will battle this to the end.

Dear Dennis,
I still think of you.

Dear Ryan,
Sex under the streetlight was a delicious accident.

Dear Kevin,
Your kiss came too late.
My lips were already dancing in the other room with Jon.

Dear Ethan,
No.

Dear Joseph,
I said you were too pretty.
They said to try it anyway.
They are fools.

Dear Avery,
You are the definition of *unrequited.*

Dear Skippy,
I'm sorry about the whiskey
and the tampon.
I'm sorry I never called you.

Dear Nate,
Until you mocked my smile, I was yours.

Dear Marc,
I like your wife too much.
Is your brother still single?

Dear Mitch,
You were my biggest mistake.
I'm sure that only makes your smile more sinister.

Dear Allen,
While you poured Guinness for Patrick,
I pictured you bending me over the bar.

Dear Graham,
I'd have swallowed that bullet.

Dear Miguel,
You said a man never forgets his first redhead.
What color are my eyes?

Dear Dennis,
I still think of you.

Dear Francis,
I'd have broken you in half.

Dear Chris,
I'm sorry I stalked you.
I'd try to forget me, too.

Dear Dex,
I can't be with you again.
Just accept it.

Dear Dr. Matthews,
No.
I'll have you fired.
Again.

Dear Aiden,
I wrote a poem about you.
It's everyone's favorite.
I find it trite.

Dear Logan,
I think I finally stopped wanting you.

Dear Cynthia,
I was drunk.
I thought you were, too.

Dear Ricky,
Maybe it was the red dress
or because I was fifteen.
Your brother married my mother
on the same day I first touched your cock.
Maybe you're still a pervert.
Call me.

Dear Jeff,
I was your biggest mistake.

Dear Robert,
You are more than beer and vomit.
You are more than I could ever put into a poem.

Dear Dennis,
I still think of you.

Dear Dennis,
I keep your photos in a box.
Each one, still in its frame.

UNSOLICITED ADVICE TO ADOLESCENT GIRLS WITH CROOKED TEETH AND PINK HAIR

When your mother hits you, do not strike back. When the boys call asking your cup size, say *A*, hang up. When he says you gave him blue balls, say *you're welcome.* When a girl with thick black curls who smells like bubble gum stops you in a stairwell to ask if you're a boy, explain that you keep your hair short so she won't have anything to grab when you head-butt her. Then head-butt her. When a guidance counselor teases you for handed-down jeans, do not turn red. When you have sex for the second time and there is no condom, do not convince yourself that screwing between layers of underwear will soak up the semen. When your geometry teacher posts a banner reading, "Learn math or go home and learn how to be a Momma," do not take your first feminist stand by leaving the classroom. When the boy you have a crush on is sent to detention, go home. When your mother hits you, do not strike back. When the boy with the blue mohawk swallows your heart and opens his wrists, hide the knives, bleach the bathtub, pour out the vodka. Every time. When the skinhead girls jump you in a bathroom stall, swing, curse, kick, do not turn red. When a boy you think you love delivers the first black eye, use a screw driver, a beer bottle, your two good hands. When your father locks the door, break the window. When a college professor writes you poetry and whispers about your tight little ass, do not take it as a compliment, do not wait, call the Dean, call his wife. When a boy with good manners and a thirst for Budweiser proposes, say *no.* When your mother hits you, do not strike back. When the boys tell you how good you smell, do not doubt them, do not turn red. When your brother tells you he is gay, pretend you already know. When the girl on the subway curses you because your tee shirt reads, "I fucked your boyfriend," assure her that it is not true. When your dog pees the rug, kiss her, apologize for being late. When he refuses to stay the night because you live in Jersey City, do not move. When he refuses to stay the night because you live in Harlem, do not move. When he refuses to stay the night because your air conditioner is broken, leave him. When he refuses to keep a toothbrush at your apartment, leave him. When you find the toothbrush you keep at his apartment hidden in the closet, leave him. Do not regret this. Do not turn red. When your mother hits you, do not strike back.

MAMA'S GIRL

When I asked about the first bruised lip,
you lied. Said he kissed you too hard.
I let that lie sit between us like a centerpiece.
Like a plump steaming turkey or shiny salted ham,
oozing its fat across the platter and down our chins.
It sat for years. Rotting. Drawing flies.
You and I politely seated on opposing sides
of the dinner table, watching the roaches swarm.
I never asked again. Used birthday money
to buy a baseball bat. Kept it under my bed,
practiced a speedy retrieval.
Our guns were useless against him.
He would've wrestled one from my small hands
long before I could steady it enough to fire.
(A baseball bat is an extra two feet of bone.
It will take a wooden door from its hinges
without alerting the neighbors.
Will take a man's leg, his shoulder.
It does not require the calm aim of injecting a bullet.
It will, however, make a man scream
just the same.)

When I was little, I had nightmares about the empty
cement room in the basement. Smaller than a closet,
no windows. Walls streaming with brown water,
moss crawling across the ceiling.
I filled that room with secrets.
Vomited all your rum into the drain on the floor.
Crammed every gummy wad of uneaten spinach

into the corners, every slap, every night
you forgot to come home.
I even put that boy with the funny name in there.
The one you took in for dinner. I baked macaroni,
told you *Geometry*, took him to the basement.
He cupped his hand over my mouth, pressed me
against the wet stink of that dungeon. We fucked like boars
while you watched Alex Trebek, cursing the tinfoil
coiled around the TV antenna.
(A boy without a home, his first day from prison,
will take any meal offered. He will nod, smile.
He will have hands thick enough for a throat.
Will leave burn marks. He will kiss so hard,
you lie.)

TERRIBLE

It is a perfect Sunday in June. There is daisy wallpaper
above the kitchen sink and a rusting Chevy pickup parked
on a dirt yard. She stands at the window, sips boxed white zinfandel,
watching as he wrestles parts off the truck. She traces a single finger
over the 19-week swell of her belly, a slow mistake, growing his eyes.

She has worn the same green $14 Walmart maternity dress
for two weeks. At the barbeque she jokes with cousins about *gaining weight.*
Cringes at his soiled shirt, clumsy tongue. They each overdrink into slurs
and spilled sauce. Argue about driving home. Once home, they do not speak.
She lies on her back, unable to turn. Pinches her eyes closed
as his hands engine across her.

In the morning, she peels crusted sheets from leaking breasts, ignores
his 9 AM beer, drives to the bank. She withdraws everything, $989.32,
Cash please, without looking up. At home, she asks him for the remaining
balance, $10.68. Asks him to come with her, hold her hand.

They age slow. Stone as statues. A year passes. Two. She asks for a divorce.
Pools of spit well in his cheeks. His arms become jackhammers. His face,
a foaming ulcer. He wrenches her to the floor, forces himself inside. Curses,
each word sharp as a wasp: *you would've been a terrible mother.*

GIRLS FOR SALE

after the portrait of a wealthy young man of considerable girth in the parlor
of his family home, labeled "Chauncey," dated 1880

The one you're asking about
came slithering up the porch steps
behind her father—
a broken man, whoring his child out for bread and coffee.

He'd groomed her to do it right, to do it all.
I would sometimes picture him giving her lessons.
She was a perfect student, mouth wide
with silence.

She washed a good floor, stitched without thimble,
never moaned beneath buckets of wood or water pails.
She nodded when she should
and didn't smile too much.
She tied my shoes, baked apples with honey.

When I told her to wipe it from my chin,
I could feel her stomach quiver beneath her blouse.
Bent above me, the stink of poverty on her breath—
I made her eat rose petals from the dining room vase.
Mother lashed her for it
and I couldn't help but laugh.

I asked her once to suck sausage grease
from my meaty fingers.
And she did.
I ate more, asked again, and she did.
Until she wretched.
I pulled her sweating hair back

from her drooling nose,
her eyes puffed with salt and fear.
I wanted to bend her in half.
The last vertebra snapping,
echoing the twig under her racing forest foot,
pulse ripping through her wrists.
Caught beneath my thumbs, she was a mouse.
Finer than painted porcelain doll-skin,
her arms blackened with bruise.

Sunday I told her to lay her head in my lap,
look up at me. *Shh—just look.*
Pearly eyes, pink lips, shining black hair.
Trembling.
With her breast in one hand,
I stroked her hair with the other.
Pulled her to my chest.
Pawing her sunken cheek,
I curled two fingers across her chin
and snapped her neck.
She fell to the floor,
so many ham-bones
sucked free of their fat.

LESSONS ON LOVING A PROPHET

1. You know how this ends.
There is nothing you can do to change it,
so make peace with it now. Ready your hands
for the callus, shred the cloth for bandages,
prepare the rosaries.

2. When you meet him, (outside the grocery,
along the boardwalk, beneath the overpass),
you will not know what he is. He will be neither
too charming, nor too handsome. Not thunder, not polish.

3. The day you fall in love, his mouth will spill
your name. He will repeat. And repeat.
He will not touch you. He will watch your hips.
Study whatever ample you have. Will ask
to watch you dance. When you turn to leave,
he will use your name like a choke chain.

4. He will call you *miracle*. Your face
will unravel. This is his magic.
When he begs you promise, say *yes*.

5. When he offers his lips, take them. Take his
arms, his throat, take his toes. When he offers,
gorge. Swallow everything whole. Gag. Vomit.
Swallow more. Do not hesitate. No time for *polite*
or *coy.*   Take.

6. When the minions call you *whore*, nod.

7. He will tell you of the others.
How they went crazy in their sleep,
awaiting his return. Do not flinch.
Do not doubt your thickened fingertips.
Stand upright. You promised.

8. When you find him in his room
thrashing the sheets, pressing his palms
into the walls, howling,
his face, a river—close the door.
This is how he makes wine.
Leave him to his sorcery.

9. When he explains how he cannot love you,
that he will never be yours alone, when he tells
how the meek and the gluttons, the tempted, the proud
are his angels—do not mourn. Smile.
Feed him. Wash his hair.

10. He is a king among thieves.
The leeches will hollow his skin, the crows,
reduce him to bones. His own heart
will empty him. Allow for the bleed. Be ready
with tourniquet and prayer.

11. In the dry burn of dawn, after the last
of the lashes, the thorns and the spittle,
when his limp body is laid at your feet,
remember the night he loved you. The ember
of his eyes and the way the words came like honey.

12. You were made for this.

METANOIA

\ˌme-tə-ˈnōi-ə\

noun

[Greek, from *metanoiein*: to change one's mind]

* a profound, usually spiritual, transformation;
* a conversion

syn: metamorphosis

BEAUTIFUL: A LEGEND

He has a bad heart.
No leaking valves, just a bad, dark purple,
slightly deflated, extra-soft heart.

I found it on the lip of the bathroom sink one morning.
I guess he left it there by accident.

I should've given it back.
But it was bad and I thought maybe I could make it un-bad.

I put it under my pillow,
thinking I could dream it into goodness.
It ruined my sheets, obviously.

I sealed it in a Ziploc bag in the refrigerator,
next to a box of baking soda to keep it fresh.
Still, after two weeks, the stench was unbearable.

I washed it off, gave it a fresh bag, moved it to the freezer.
It iced over within a few days and I was terribly
worried about freezer burn.

Finally, I pickled it in a mason jar.
I carry it with me in my bag
alongside all my books and asthma inhalers,
between my favorite poets' poems.

He hasn't come asking for it.
I guess he has no idea where he left it.
Maybe he grew a new one.

✝

She was twelve years old the first time.
But since she didn't say *yes*, she doesn't count it.
The boy's friends stood in the window and watched. They cheered.
Cords bound her wrists, a boy inside her new body.
The tallest of the faces from the other side of the glass,
whooping and hollering, his blonde bangs flapping as he jumped
and applauded. All his glee, watching her two skinny legs
thrash like that.

She started counting.
The chubby boy with the thicket of black curls,
the one with the blue mohawk and armfuls of tattoos,
the Greek one she eventually married and divorced,
she counted all of them.

Most times, she wanted it. Most times, she was hoping for it.
Some say she was filling up whatever hole that first boy left.
(That's what they say.) She only knows that most times,
she was hoping for it and most times, they gave it to her.

Sometimes she didn't want it but already had the gift of knowing
what happens when you say *no*. She took to saying *yes*.
She took to whiskey. So long as it burned.
This made the *yes* easier.

She did, eventually, lose count.

Manipulative types used words like *always* and *love*.
The gullible used words like *damage* and *repair*.
The word *friends* became synonymous with *cannibals*
after Friend crammed a fat hand down her jeans while she slept
and Friend pulled back her vomit hair and crawled up her passed-out thighs
and Friend brought along three other Friends and together,
they pulled her arms straight off her ragdoll body.
(If you look close you can see where she stitched them back on.)

The people made up stories, called them facts.
They stoned her with silence.
Used her name to scold their children.
Today, she lives alone
in a city with a happy name.
She keeps marvelous houseplants,
wears war paint on her legs.
She refuses to speak; writes notes in Braille
on paper napkins with knitting needles. Rumor has it,
she pickled her last lover's heart
in a mason jar.
Carries it around with her
everywhere.

CARNIVORES
for Eboni Hogan

She is the prettiest thing New York City
has seen since Christmas.
It is 2:38 AM. We have matching boots,
swirl cheap red wine between half-glossed lips,
jab bent forks into hard falafels.
The night is ready to end its shift.

A plump waitress wears the city's tightest
electric-pink sweater, (a Valentine for her beloved).
Two Marines wink from February's side of the glass,
a king cockroach lies wait in the ladies room sink,
the swordfish on the butcher block is looking for his gullet.

It is raining Merlot.
Our construction paper hearts, soaked
all the way through.

It's 2:38 AM, and I am stuffing her with confession.
She sucks the fat, licks her fingers.
I am gutted and we are ravenous, eating with our hands:
slurp, chew, gnash. Gluttons.

Soon, the bar and the second bottle are empty.

I watch her take the dull blade of a table knife
to her chest, (my jaw hanging loose like a broken
screen door swinging in a summer monsoon).
She slices straight through her breast,
breaks off two ribs, sets them on her plate—
blood rivering through the hummus.

She takes my hand, jabs my curious fingers
into the wound. I dig in hard,
all the way up to my elbow.

She doesn't even wince.

The cooks across the room scorch
something that once was alive.
The pink waitress brings us each a free glass
of whatever wine is left and extra napkins
to mop up the pooling red spill
from our lips.

UNTRUTH

after Daniel McGinn

My daughter and I are chopping apples. She's a good washer, scrubs the rinds until they squeak. (We bake our pies skin-on.) She measures everything into ramekins like on TV and pretends we are chefs on a cooking show. When she looks away, I sneak extra cinnamon in with the sugar. She scolds me if I don't follow the recipe exactly, asserting that *baking is chemistry and precise measurements are key! We must not be foolish!* Sometimes she talks like my grandmother. She's 5 years old and gives *me* the giggles. Sundays here are fresh. Golden.

Once the pie is in the oven, she watches cartoons and ends up napping. The dog lies with her, rubbing his snout into her red curls. My scrapbooks are filled with pictures of them like that. I clean the flour off the counter and wash the dishes, starting on dinner slowly, knowing she'll want to wash the tomatoes before I chop them. Just after I pull the pie out to cool, she waddles into the kitchen with a fat yawn, rubbing her eyes. I give her a glass of soy milk. *What did you dream about?*

She's grouchy when she wakes up (just like me), so she doesn't answer, only reaches for the tomatoes and starts scrubbing. When I look up, she is 41, taking a long pull on a cigarette. She gestures for the ashtray and returns to washing tomatoes. She is drunk. I am 12 and there is no pie. But the dishes are clean and she talks like my grandmother, who is her mother, clipping hard on the "r" in *warshing the vegetables.*

Soon, she is cursing and hurling dishes. There is a hot sting in my cheekbone and a purple swell. I finish making dinner while she watches Miami Vice. Pray she doesn't pass out before her boyfriend shows up to rub his snout in my hair.

GOD REPLIES.
after selected USA Today "Pictures of the Day" 2008

Bodies line a path to a Hindu temple in India after a human stampede.
   I gave you faith.
   I gave you fear.
   I gave you feet.

Children play on a jungle gym in Kabul, Afghanistan.
   I never get thank you notes.

A five-year-old earthquake victim is fitted for an artificial arm
in Chengdu, China.
   You ask where I was when the earth shook,
   when that giant mouth cracked open,
   when the great crush plucked their limbs like flower petals.
   Love me, love me not...

A Palestinian youth punches an Israeli police officer in the West Bank.
   At the tip of each arm,
   a ravenous fist. His curse, your sweat.
   There is milk and earth and wool.
   There is wine and machinery. There is religion. Bullet. Gunsmoke.
   I gave you fists.
   Marvel.

An elderly couple escapes from their home in Kvemo-Achabeti, Georgia
after it was set on fire by Russian militia.
   He carries her firm on his back. Takes all of her,
   wolf mother to cub, scruff in the teeth.
   She will ride until his spine folds beneath them.
   Together they will run.   And run.
   I gave them feet.

A five-year-old girl kisses her mother goodbye on her first day
of kindergarten in Springfield, Ohio.
    I never get thank you notes.

A family hauls their belongings through floodwater in Nepal
after a dam breaks on the Koshi River.
    You ask where I was when the rock cracked,
    when the single drop of riverwater became five,
    became twenty, became a wall.
    Tomorrow, your fins will turn back to thumbs,
    officials will deny, engineers confess.

Russian soldiers inspect a car carrying a coffin at a checkpoint
near Zugdidi, Georgia.
    Their sneer is terror. Their ankles will bend. Their guns will rust.
    One day, they will carry coffins of their own.
    On that day, they will pray.
    On that day, I will fill their ears
    with your names.

Six Iraqi children watch a US soldier search their house.
    Twelve hushed eyes swarm and bulge and swallow
    the steel arm of rifle, the dust on your helmet,
    stubble of your chin.
    Twelve eyes that can never un-see you.
    I gave you eyes.
    You have already
    forgotten their faces.

Palestinian children fly kites on a Gaza City beach.
    I never get thank you notes.

Burqa-clad Afghan women wait on a cart.
    I made you perfect.
    Gave you eyes. Fists.
    Feet.

HOLY
for Jon Sands

Sometimes we eat each other's lettuce
straight off the plate. Or french fries,
or whole halves of sandwiches, drink wine
(and whiskey) from the bottle, add hot sauce
to *everything*. Sit on the floor in the poetry aisle
at Barnes & Noble, the lady with sharp points on her feet
carefully overstepping spread fingers, the nanny sighing a heavy
infuriation as the six-year-old in her charge whines,
but THEY'RE on the ground!, and we have never been this holy.
Not even those nights on the chewing gum steps
of Union Square exchanging epic stories about girls with butterfly
wings and boys made of turpentine until the sweet arc of dawn
bronzes this city's rusty skyline, the sticky grip of *holy* cradling us,
belly-up, like sunstroke, like a wriggling pup, like a god we sit
cynically disbelieving but laughing with over late-night beers.
This is the stink of *forgive me*, the shirt drenched in sweat
and sometimes sobs. This is what it means to have love.
There is nothing in you that says *hold me*, no unfolding bulb
of flutter; this is not the agonizing thrum of heartache,
not the tricky misgivings of future; this is the answer
to why we came, why we stay, why each morning
is a reason, and why *friend* is the weakest word between us.
You glance across the table, smile in the knowing
that I, too, will never eat meat (wouldn't matter, but I won't)
and it's easy. How I know we will walk, regardless the rain or the ice,
there is no room for taxi, for subway, when four good calves
and a long conversation are the only measure of distance
between Eighth Avenue and the Lower East Side.
How I know you'll always come home, always, even when home
means riverbed or volcano or passenger seat of a 1993 Camry

or floorboards in a bookstore where you read poems aloud to me
from Rosal's *My American Kundiman* until we are belly-up drooling
and a six-year-old boy witnesses holy
for the first time.

PLUM

I kept him in a birdcage
in my closet for months

brought him rice and seeds (when I remembered)
sometimes water, a sip of warm soda

once, as I was pulling tulips
from the rose bed, he escaped

returned days later in silk lavender, unfurled his smile
like a clothesline full of crisp spring bed sheets

that night I cut a small incision four inches
below my collarbone, retrieved a plum

rinsed it, locked it
in the cage beside him

by morning, my closet
was a jungle of plum trees

saplings pushing up through floorboards, branches sprouting
from the door jamb, juice streaming down the walls

I climbed the tallest of the trees, hung the cage
from its highest branch, opened the latch

as he hopped onto my finger,
I pressed my lips to his feathery face

I reached in, snatched the purple fruit
dug my thumbs into the plump

tore it in two

THE GREAT HUSH
after the parting

At the dinner party, nine near-strangers crowd around
a table two sizes too small, sipping on wine and dipping
morsels into sauces, chatting about 1970s films and the
proper methods for chopping beets and salting pork. After
the first course, someone mentions your name. The room
falls to a hush. (Poor fool has no idea what he has done.)
The wine in the glasses begins to rise, the flatbread unrolls
and butters itself, napkins fall to the floor, a lobster claw
reaches up and snaps off the tip of a man's nose. The wine
continues rising up over the lip of each glass, a trout's eye
winks at its fork, the chickens in the kitchen cluck and
stretch their featherless wings, soup springs from a boy's
spoon back into his bowl. The wine soaks through the
tablecloth, dripping red pearls onto each tightly-packed
thigh. When I clear my throat to answer, the clams on
one woman's plate pop up, slap shut their shells and scuttle
off across the floor, down Madison Avenue, and from what
I can tell, straight back out to the sea.

PEACH

Often, the poems dress up in third person. Or I say
pomegranate when I mean *the rat in Apartment H
who flirts with little boys and shows me his wiener
in the elevator.* It's a puzzle. Play with me.

I know a fella who leaves surprise notes for me
in obscure places, (subway doors, Times Square bill-
boards, between the pages of cooking magazines
at the Barnes & Noble checkout). Usually just advice.

Little gems like fortune-cookie fortunes or anecdotes
about shotguns. Once, a recipe for tacos. Sometimes
they're meant for others. Girls mostly. Pick-up lines
or pictures of dolls in knee-highs with spread legs.

There's another fella. He backed into my living
room with a garbage truck a few years ago. Visits
every few months to repair the walls. It's slow going.
I live on the third floor and he doesn't have a ladder.

I sometimes wish he would leave me notes. Or at
least bring a vacuum. Instead, he tells panty-slinging
college girls that he's got a problem with honesty
and bourbon. They line up outside his trailer

with gel pens and open shirts, contemplating what
to ask him to scribble across their boobs. Once
in a while he gets bubble gum stuck in his beard
and I think, *Hmm, not really "Daddy" material.*

The last fella composes full-length love letters
and appeared in six of the last seven episodes
of *Get it Right* (that sitcom where the perpetual
commitmentphobe lands the nutcase girlfriend).

His letters arrive by carrier pigeon. I never write
back because the practice of using animals where
a simple email would suffice seems extravagant.
I untie the notes from their little pink legs,

offer a handful of seeds, shoo them off my ledge.
I read the letters by candlelight, find baby names
written between each apology. Last night, I dreamed
I was pregnant, couldn't decide who I should ask

to marry. Woke up in a new borough, cranky
as a rattlesnake. Today, my favorite word is *peach.*
It means *the daisy in Apartment D who broke
her lip open on the first boy she didn't kiss.*

THE LAMB
after artist Angie Mason

I.
she used gardening shears to open her last lover's chest
green smudges staining the rungs of each rib

started at his abdomen, face-first
tearing at the new meat, *yank, chew, pull*
a frightening scene, those long cords of intestine snaking
into her mouth, tendons swinging from her jowls

she slept for three days
woke craving a strawberry milkshake

II.
on her way back from the creamery, she passed a farmhouse
the fenced yard sprawling with playful spring lambs

she snatched one for her purse
he was soft as clouds, wriggling and bleating
she couldn't wait to get him home and tie ribbons in his wooly hair

he wobbled into the kitchen curious as a suitor
moved his sad moon eyes up into hers
folded his ears backward, whispered
anything for you

III.
it was three more lambs before she was done
there was a mighty, steaming mess in the compost heap
flies, rats, and stray dogs circling

she busied herself in the parlor with scissors and thread
cutting and measuring, gutting and sewing, working tirelessly

days later, finally completed
she slipped into the new suit, stitched the hood
right onto her own cheeks
grinned

the boys will never recognize me like this

BUTCHER

CUTTERS

His eyes are drooping bloodhounds. The bridge of his nose
bends to the side, a permanent whistle. His left fist is a bullet.
When he was ten, he found his mother hanging in the closet
beside her favorite blue sundress. His father broke his nose
eight times in three years. You discovered him under his own
face. He kisses you hard. Butchers your lips. Says your carved
arms are sculptures. Says he will cut them off one day, mount
them on a mannequin like Kali. You are fifteen and he fits like a
key. Your mother is on the floor again. Smells like turpentine,
wears her newest lover like spandex. His gunmetal is refuge. He
sketches you, feeds you poems. Cuffs you to the wall, plants
dark lilacs into your cheekbones. Explains how he held the
others down, fingered them as they choked. How their eyes grew
fat as plums. When he tries to open your throat with a chef's
knife, you leave your shoes behind. Find a cab. A new name.
A new city. Twenty years later, you peel your children from the
pet shop window, tell them *no, we can't bring home that cute
little bloodhound.*

THE DOLLS

for Elisabeth Fritzl

Josef Fritzl imprisoned his daughter Elisabeth in the cellar of their home for 24 years.
Among countless other abuses, he repeatedly raped her, resulting in the birth of seven
children.

"The cellar in my building belonged to me and me alone — it was my kingdom..."
— *Josef Fritzl*

I built you a brood.
Used a tiny hammer and miniature chisels,
smoothed each little elbow with sandpaper,
hinged their joints with twine and wire
clipped from hangers.
Gave them button eyes and marshmallow lips,
made their clothes from tissue and the string
I once pulled from a pigeon's nest.

Six perfect toy soldiers, just for you.
Seven, if you count the one in the incinerator.
He was blue as a robin's egg. His limbs,
limp as an un-strung marionette.
When you burned him, our home bloomed
with the scent of chicory and cloves
like Christmas.

The six survivors
hanging from my breasts
do not know my name.

The three you took away
use the word *lost* as if wandering
the supermarket or a parking lot.

Yet there they were: perched canaries
at grandmother's window,
slurping spiced pumpkin soup,
calling you *Uncle*,
wearing their faces inside-out.

The three you left in the dungeon with me
have grown into ghosts.
Veal calves, raised without sunlight,
born for slaughter.
They stroke the rats like puppies,
play hide and seek with roaches,
eat each other's scabs.

You clever craftsman,
built me a doll house.
Turned me into doll maker.

Puppets with hinged jaws,
painted lashes that never blink,
porcelain hands, wooden feet,
and Father, look!
they all have your eyes.

MEN

want to fix you
save you
or fuck you

I can't be fixed
and I don't care to be saved

THE COLLECTION

after artist Tyson Schroeder

Tuesday, making dinner for my love
at his stove, I reach to the cupboard
looking for oregano,
hoping for peppercorns
(the sauce will fail without them)
but find instead each shelf
crammed with old jelly jars,
rinsed clean and resealed.
Labeled by hand with exquisite
penmanship: *Thighs, Toes, Fingernails,*
Glossed Lips, Hair, Noses, Pierced Earlobes.
I pull them slowly into the light,
turn the jars in my hands.
Everything so small, as if
from thimble-sized women.
Swatches of braided hair in every color;
whole ascending sets of perfectly-painted
toes; pairs of weeping eyes in hazel,
brown, and blue. Then, in the back,
a lonely jar. Dark red with a meaty pulp
and what appear to be small black cherries
pressing their shiny heads against the glass.
Labeled, *Unborn.*

YELLOWFEATHER

He brought home a pit bull one night.
An angry prizefighter, just for you.
You made him lock the *ugly fucking
thing* in the garage. It was summer.
Days over 90 degrees. He never came
back for the dog. We waited. No light.
No air. One small broken pane on the
window. I wedged paper bowls of cat
food through it so he wouldn't die. He
grew thin, mean, lonely as an eclipse.
After two months, you called Animal
Control. Made me answer the officer
from behind a locked door, give him
all the right lies: *No, he is not our dog.
The owner's name is Arlo Yellowfeather.
Yes, Native American. 35. Male. No, he
does not live here. No, the dog does not
obey me. No, I cannot reach the owner.
No, my parents are not home.* He used
a control rod to drag the filthy, snarling,
twisting ribcage across the yard, into
the alley. Then the hard thud of a dart.
A wretched howl. I sobbed for hours.
Spent the next two weeks scrubbing
blood and shit off the brick walls of the
garage. Ten years later, he appears by his
real name in the Sunday paper. Indicted
for murder. Left the bleeding woman in
a field in Montana. They found her solid
as a popsicle. Stuck, like chewing gum.

WHAT YOU WILL CARRY

Outstretched, she is just a body for fishes.
You hold all her heavy,
suspended above the greedy water,
just burden, one wrong turn among the rest.
You are alone at the bank and the river
is whispering its invitation,
the *trickle*, the *hum rush swirl*.
It serenades the rocks and the wood,
carefully bathes the reeds and dead things.
Wash wash pull splash and back again.
The water *comes* and *comes*, as long as there is
axis and ocean, it will never stop *coming*, here
to your feet.
Your toes in the rocks are white marbles,
round and elegant, how the water licks
over and *over*, savors the smallest of your skin.
Your hands are loosing their grip now,
the river is opening the girl's weight.
She is not waking up, she is head loll
and tumble hair, your muscles weaken with
her heavying mass, each strand linked to its tendon,
tendon to bone, you are shuddering.
She is slipping now and you try to release
but she multiplies, her face is twenty faces,
they clutch at your arms, frantic,
dragging at your calves, your ankles, kicking
the water's face like an advancing dog
like a boy with too much knuckle. Your name
is rust in each of their mouths and you cannot sink them,
there will never be river enough to wash them away.

THE CUT

pry open the legs

        this is no lover

reach inside

        this empty casket

the red soft

        satin mouth of me

up to the womb

        this fiery magic sack

finger the hard

        yellow knots

like callus, he said

        welded to the Gate

        ✝

take the scalpel

        cut

painless

        open-eyed-wild

sink the yellow beads

        into formaldehyde

paste the wound closed

        blood urine

aftershocks

        the cut

inside

        shaped like a seed

lab results read

        like prayers

forgive the Sin

        of woman

    wearing gender on the inside

benign, he said

I heard, *survive*

CLEAVE

in memory of Betty Leah LaGrow

He plopped it down like a mound of bad pudding
but it settled upright, a proud cupcake,
skin still prickling like gooseflesh,
the brown button at its peak popping up
like a thermometer from a perfectly broiled
rump roast, saluting the way it did for clumsy
school boys behind the library under thick
pink sweaters, a gumdrop even the anesthesiologist
wanted to pop into her mouth.

AND/OR

It's been years since we dated and he is like a brother and I trust his laughter and I just vomited in the ladies room at JP Horgan's off the 7 train and we stumble to my apartment and sleep and I am still drunk when his fingers wake me from inside and I know I didn't say *yes* and I know I didn't say anything (because I was asleep) and I know I should say *no* now and I blame the eighth beer and I blame the free shot of Jaeger and blame is easier than stopping him so *go, go, take* and I'll just tuck into the corner and watch him and wait and finally he finishes and finally I can go back to sleep and then a radio alarm goes off and we walk to the train and I hug him goodbye and he's just an old friend again and I go to my Midtown cubicle and avoid mirrors and avoid conversation and go home again and shower again and love him still because he's like a brother and *love* him still and blame that girl, the one in the towel on the floor with the anemic blue marks all over her thighs, blame that girl, blame her, the one who wears my name like a scuffed pair of boots, uses it like a revolving door

or hold lovers like birth marks or use ash like perfume or empty the bottle or cradle the girls who polish my rusty name or forget to call him on his birthday or strangle the blue raccoon dog toy until the squeak breaks or curse the stranger who bumps me on the subway or swallow salt or break the lock or plunge boot into plaster or take up cigarettes again or congratulate him when he moves in with his next apology or slam fist to desktop or buy a glitter cell phone cover or wear plaid mini skirts or let the dog's fur go matted or buy an extra round just so they'll stay or miss the train or ignore phone calls or wear a groove into the barstool at JP Horgan's or go to work on weekends or masturbate until my calves ache or have doctors prescribe sedatives I'll never take or buy self help books I'll forget to read or sleep until 2 in the afternoon or hold a baby to see if I can keep from crying or walk by his apartment at 3 in the morning or wear eyeliner for the first time in years or gorge on macadamia nut chocolates or finally forgive that girl, the one with the scuffed boots, the one with the marble smile.

This is not courage.
This is a girl with too much fist. Never enough soap.
This is trying to hold the moon because he is the only one without hands.

FIREFLIES

CROSS THE SEA, ESMAN.

for Esman Greene

On June 19, 2008, Jamaican immigrant Esman Greene died on the floor of the emergency room waiting area at New York City's Kings County Psychiatric Ward. Diagnosed as paranoid schizophrenic, she had been hospitalized against her will and without her family's consent. She lay dead in full view of hospital staff for over an hour, as captured by cameras.

I.   *On the third day God created America.*

Dyed the thread blue. Stitched a patchwork
banner, tourniquets, blindfolds.

There were men, parchments, there were wives
and cattle. Gospels covered in lambskin.

God brought sea cargo with hollow eyes, saltwater lungs
made rivers and beasts and mountains for conquering.

Offered handcuffs, needles, built waiting rooms.
There was a woman, sticky like dried fruit.

The zookeeper watched.
Smiled when her rat-legs twitched.

II.   *Esman becomes America.*

You are gravel scratch shoes,
crows' cackle, hissing power lines,
the rumble of an elevated train
grinding through Brooklyn.
You are faucet drip, chirping cell phone,
firework's snap, barista latte foam,

playground chatter, iron bars clanked with keys,
a shotgun crack. You are blooded coughs,
bile splash, schizophrenic's howl
after the injection.

III. *Jamaica calls on weekends.*

First, they promise you a dream:
Cross the sea, Esman.

You leave your country.
Find a church, a bed, a lampshade.
You work, send money and gifts to six waiting mouths,
their toes digging into the sand you regret.

When the tics start, you call it a phase.
When the voices arc, you buy a bottle of chardonnay.
You lose your job, close the sun from your room, forget how to eat.
By the time the clocks start to scream,
you've forgotten your eldest daughter's name.

They break the lock. Bind your limbs.
Tuck their tongues behind the word *healers.*
When the fluid bites into your blood, the lights go grey.
When the floor kisses your cheekbone, your mouth curls into fist
but you are mute, blind, alone   in a room of warm corpses.

IV. *Said the manic to the muse.*

Sweet Esman, I have opened my skin
countless times.
Choked on the gristle picked from your plate,
muted the voices with pills and wine.
Smashed the clocks, Esman,
smashed them!

Kings County will place you on the mantle they forgot to build.
They'll frame you without glass on a wall with no paint,
repent with each pluck of a new vein.

When they place your bones on the ship,
push off from the dock, when the wind carries your sweet bloom
across the sea, through the palms,
when the sand finally welcomes you home,

America will be here
waving.

THE WITCHES
(a love song)
for RM, MM, COA, MB, LP

They pick at New York City's
pockmark face. Push rusted shopping
carts rattling with sticky tin heartsick.

Hit me again, fucker, touted by each
lovely jawbone. Fifty knuckles crack—
melody blooming from under chipped polish.

Each mouth unique in its cradle of the word
poem. Wishbone eulogies for chickadees
crushed in their fists: teeth picked with feathers,

blooded talons used for handmade doll's feet.
(Children gnaw as a pup would its squeak toy.)
They wind fingers around invisible harp strings,

cast spells between batted lashes, tuck smirks
beneath tongues, drag leashes without dogs,
suckle anything with a heartbeat.

But if it refuses the milk, loop the leash
around its neck, tie it to a post, sing: *rain-
drops on roses and whiskers on kittens,*

sweetly, while it starves. Dangle
the carcass above the next waiting
litter of hungry chirping hounds.

EXIT WOUND

You are an exit wound,

the extra shot of tequila,

the tangled knot of hair that must be cut out.

You are the cell phone ringing in a hushed theatre,

pebble wedged in the sole of a boot,

the bloody hangnail.

You are, *just this once.*

You are flip-flops in a thunderstorm,

the boy's lost erection,

a pen gone dry.

You are my father's nightmare,

my mother's mirage.

You are a manic high.
(Which is to say:
you are a bad idea.)

You are herpes despite the condom.

You are, *I know better.*

You are pieces of cork floating in the wine glass.

You are the morning after,
(whose name I can't remember,
still in my bed).

The hole in my rain boots,

vibrator with no batteries.

You are, *shut up and kiss me.*

You are naked wearing socks,

mascara bleeding down laughing cheeks,

the wrong guy buying me a drink.

You are the typo in an otherwise brilliant novel,

sweet-talk into unprotected sex,

the married coworker,

my stubbed toe.

You are not new or uncommon,

not brilliant or beautiful.

You are a bad idea.

(Rock star in the back seat of a taxi,
burned popcorn,
top shelf, at half price.)

An exit wound.

A word I cannot translate.

A name I cannot say.

The poem I cannot write.

You are everything I want.

NUMEROLOGY

78   - the number of cows slaughtered every minute in the U.S.
100   - my score on every spelling test I've ever taken
4   - the number of wedding rings my mother has pawned
16,200 - the amount of money I've had to borrow from my father to
          pay your debt
115   - my weight when I met you
245   - your weight when you first purged a dinner
97   - the number of times you told me I was fat
24   - the number of beers you drank each day
136   - my weight when you stopped touching me
135   - the weight of your emaciated six-foot frame today
17   - the number of times you refused to get help
21   - the number of days since our divorce
76   - the number of cows slaughtered since the beginning of this
          poem

PRESUMPTION

it looked like the taste
        of my boyfriend's tongue
I wrote
in a poem once
and the quasi-psycho
art-is-free
        life-is-pain
                poet-slam-artist
from class
named *Alarm Clock*
said,
"Mmm, I thought you were
                lesbian,
        for some reason."
that night
I dreamed about fucking Mr. Clock

next class
        I did

he dropped the class
        took an F
and I trashed his babble poetry
in the Cans Only bin
outside room 233

recently
I heard he was
strung
        out
                hard
on heroin

that night
I fucked a woman

THE WORST THING I EVER TAUGHT A GIRL

In the spring of the last year
we were together,
I walked your niece to the playground
down the block from your brother's house.
There was sun and moss.
I pushed her on the swings,
sprang from bent knees on the teeter-totter,
climbed with her over the monkey bars.

We sat together then
on a long stretch of railroad tie
at the base of the playground, near the creek.
We were careful of the splinters.
She asked me if I loved you and I said *yes.*
She asked if we were going to get married and I laughed.
Not a gleeful laugh, nor one of spite, just a giggle
as wickedly innocent as each of her seven years.

I don't know, I said,
that's up to your uncle.

GRAHAM

Three years.
A flat-black
punk-rock
love-mobile
Dodge Dart.
Tattoos and
blue hair—
your
nicotine taste
made me high.
We moved in a
slow-mo frame
of hardcore and
hallucination.
Smirnoff
was our rummy
partner.
On special
occasions,
Southern Comfort.
And it was fun.
Until the
psych ward
at Porter
Memorial—
slashed wrists
and liver
rot. After
two years
of detox

and Hide-
the-Booze,
I quit.
You didn't.
And I'm sorry
it was
Christmas
but I had
to go.

UNREQUITED

You will hold her hand,
raise your son,
play basketball,
eventually become
professor of something
stiffly mathematical,
climb respectably out of debt,
cry at your son's college graduation,
drink Scotch,
murmur about losing weight.

I will write poems
you'll never read.

MOTHER, IF IN A MUSEUM
after an artist's digital rendering, titled, "Medea"

*"I shall leave the land and flee from the murder of my dear children and I
shall have done a dreadful deed."*
    — Medea, by Euripides, 431 BC

An artist butchered your face. Genius.
The curators mounted it in a massive gold baroque frame.
Hung it on a white wall in the new corridor of the south wing.
You.
Five feet wide and me, small as my own freckles,
staring up at the huge canvas.
Your crater eyes dance in a way they never did down here on the ground.
I bet you just love your new immortality.
I must admit, I yelped.
Startling, those jutting cheekbones.
The yellowed skin blended with sweet peach,
then dragged down with what must have been rakes.
Blond eyelashes hacked away, even a bleaching
for your nicotine teeth. Impressive, Ma.
So monstrous. Alone on that forty-foot wall.

You're so permanent
like that.

LULLABY (REPRISE)

RACING HUMMINGBIRDS

after mania

she owns three   light bulbs

    all in use
         filaments ready   to burst

days litter   beer bottles
    and
      unopened prescriptions

legs open, simple as an envelope
she is filled
with Dear John letters

her laughter   arcs

    above the bar fight

this
sickness,

this is how a woman
        becomes

    a wing

SWARM

Learn how to say "no."

Cram that word inside your mouth,
the whole thing, make sure all of it
gets in there. Let it walk on your tongue.
Practice with it in the mirror, push it
out, make faces, learn to love the salt
and bitter of it. Teach it to perch on your lip,
buzz, collect pollen from your sugary gloss.
Make it swarm between your cheeks.

Then, when the days come (there will be
many) where he pushes too hard, speaks
too sweetly, when the hand at your thigh
draws a thump in your stomach, when
the bitch gremlin inside whispers *it's not
worth the fight*, says you can barter
for your worth tomorrow, when your ribs
shrink, when he unfurls his Almighty Smile,
when four come at you at once, when
you love someone else, when the bar
is closing and your name becomes *Take
What I Can Get*, when the girls hate you
anyway, when you want him until the burn
if only he wore a different face—

pull back your lips, bare the teeth you have
sharpened to their perfect points, flick
your stinger tongue, set free your swarm.

THIS IS HOW

This is how married wakes,
pulls back the sheets,
stumbles into its day.

This is how married eats breakfast.
How it commutes to work, makes dinner,
walks the dog.
This is how married has sex,
(after the late show every Wednesday).

This hollow hand hold,
this systematic push of the cart;
dairy aisle, produce, deli:
¼ *lb Swiss*, *2 loaves baguette*.

This is how married pays the mortgage,
(a week late, waiting for payroll).
This is how it forgets to mow the lawn,
lets the dishes pile up.

This is how married fumbles through cocktail parties,
misplaced glances at the sunken cleavage,
the well-groomed bachelor.
This is how it drinks too much,
wipes up the vomit,
this is how married laughs about it later.

This empty kiss,
this practiced fold and zip of business luggage,
ring slipped into a pocket at the hotel bar.
This is how married commits,

(the accident, the *I didn't mean to*
whispered nameless the morning after).

This is how married neglects.
Buries itself under prescription bottles,
video games, shower masturbation,
shopping sprees.
This is how married goes into debt.

Holiday cards signed, "we."
(The all-powerful unit, unflinching.)
We hope you…, we wish you…,
we lie.

This gasp and ache,
this is how it feels the first time you ask him to leave.
How it feels to say, *I will always love you,*
pray he believes.

This is how it feels to hurl the ring across the room.

How it feels the next time you ask him to leave.

This is how you reclaim your name.
How you label the box, "wedding photos."
How you file bankruptcy.
How you tell your father you failed.
How you cry when they explain *you will owe alimony.*

This is how it feels the last time he pushes inside you,
his sobs falling down your throat, your voice saying, *no.*

This is how it feels the last time you ask him to leave.

And this—

this is how it feels
when he does.

RESURRECTION

In 1981 Charles Chatman was wrongfully convicted of rape.
Imprisoned for nearly 27 years, he was released January 4, 2008, after DNA evidence
proved his innocence.

Charles Chatman to his accuser:

I've been writing this letter for 9,850 days.

9,850 drafts, etched into the walls of an 8' x 8' cell.

9,850 yellow stench mornings,
how swift they come.

The latch,
the echo of bars against concrete.

Some would lay lilies at my feet.

Do you know what happens
to a black man
in a Texas prison
convicted of raping a white woman?

I wanted to carve your face in the floor,
get you out from behind my eyelids.

"That's him."

Your little finger twitched
on the soft trigger.

Boom.

You let your rapist go free.

Fingered me from the line up.
You had known my face for 13 years,
growing up on the same street.

*Tell me, did you wear lilies in your hair
on your wedding day?*

I served more time than any other
of the Texas damned.

Alibi, ignored.
Skin, convicted.

But where ethics and justice failed me,
I was rescued by science.

Still, they say I *won* my freedom.
(In the lottery of caged men.)

Tonight, I will sleep on fresh sheets,
my aunt's fluffed pillows.
I will eat cheeseburgers on a free tongue.

I will not know my family
or the world around me.

Won't recognize my aunt's calloused hands,
my father's gravestone.

I will have no history to talk about at dinner parties,
no wife's discerning glance,
no walk down a daughter's wedding aisle,
no resume to employ.

The skills I've learned have no place in an office or a library,
anywhere without Plexiglas windows
and razor wire.

At 47,
I am a blank page.

Those who would lay lilies at my feet know
there is no resurrection here.

ERASER

✝

The brown dots dance like Brazil,
like Irish feet after whiskey,
like a teen girl drunk on her own plaid miniskirts
and the sweet smell of the spike-haired boy in Algebra.
There is dirt in those freckles.
There are stories and insult, there is shame
the size of Central Park or your boss' SUV
or even the Atomic Bomb.

My mother, as a child, takes sandpaper to her own cheeks,
scrubs with cotton balls dipped in bleach,
hides beneath scarves and long-sleeves in summer.

At 7, her grandpa praises those freckles, kisses each one.
Kisses and kisses   and kisses
far into the stretches of skin without freckles.
At 10, she tells herself that the wonder of a redhead
is one even grandfathers cannot resist.
At 13, she is a galaxy of dancing spots,
the blonde girls tell her she is ugly, the boys
who receive her valentines call her names.
By 18, she has married the first man to ever say she was pretty,
easy bride for the backhand.
By 29, she is giving birth to another man's baby,
divorce papers spread across the table,
this new man has a ring in his pocket.
By 40, she is alone, save the daughter she didn't intend.
By 45, she is passed out on the front porch.
She is passed out in a bathroom stall.
She is screwing on a pool table

in front of the freckle-faced daughter she never wanted.
She is vomiting as the daughter holds back her hair.
She is punching the freckle-faced daughter.
She is erasing the freckle-faced daughter
and the men and the valentines and the red hair
and the whole   galaxy.

✝

A man who has just had a final shot of tequila, (one shot too
many), who figures the drive is short and there is no traffic
and the only thing on these dark country roads after midnight
are deer and the occasional skunk, who then cries when one
striped little beast rolls under his tire, and though the blood
washes off in the next rain, the skunk smell pushes up through
the vents every time he turns up the heat,
probably half-praises an unnamed god that it was not another
car—a car filled with names and birthdates and photo albums,
half-happy it was "just" a lurking midnight animal.

A pregnant woman who does not want to be pregnant, (who will
soon no longer be pregnant), but who, for now, and for the next
two weeks, must lie only on her back, must graduate unwillingly
into Walmart maternity wear, must fold Kleenex into perfect
squares to absorb the milk from her leaking breasts,
probably wonders the color of her fetus's eyes, counts the number
of freckles across a nose she will never kiss.

✝

The galaxies undo themselves,
unravel from their gravitational
architecture. Whole stars fall limp,
molecules deconstruct and implode,
atoms simply dissolve.

You rip pages from your journal.
Put your toothbrush in your pocket, leave the apartment
unlocked, board a train with a one-way ticket.

The boy with the broken heart
cuts the wings from the bird he has starved in a cage.

The redhead takes scissors to her stubborn hair.

I Photoshop the freckles off my cheeks in photographs,
write poems to the unborn.

CHIME

after the plagiary

Sometimes the soy milk sits in the Starbucks refrigerator too long
and when they add it to my latte (once in a while I treat myself
to a gaudy latte with trimmings) it collects at the bottom, not unlike
cottage cheese, so I ask them to re-make it and I become, again, *that* girl.

Sometimes people screw up.
Sometimes I am the mistake.
Sometimes when I look at their boots (covered in my blood) I still try
to convince myself that I was kicked by someone else.

Sometimes I am just a girl with wounded poems and a bright laugh
who likes cheap beer and pink polka dots, who winces
when her friends argue and cannot bring herself to love.

Sometimes I lace up damage like boxing gloves.
Sometimes I kick the doors of New York City taxi cabs.
Sometimes I curse at pizza shop owners.

Sometimes your husband is a wretch and you are misery and wine
becomes your bedmate. Soon then, new lovers, and you polish them
with a kindness you didn't know you had and wash their hairless
backs with thick wet teardrops, sometimes you fuck your boss
or blacken your fist on a moving windshield.

Sometimes *you* takes the place of *I*.

Sometimes you write poems. Sometimes a man behind a computer
screen asks you to prove that a *Miguel* is really a *Miguel*, and that
there is still a man in Colorado looking for you with his fists and his
hammer claw and this is why you changed his name in the story,

and that Graham's ashes are kept in a copper urn on his mother's
mantle, that you've cradled the damn thing in your own hands—
Yes, it's all real, sir, those love letters are mine!

Sometimes I delete messages without listening to them.
Sometimes I take too long to reply to emails.
Sometimes I drink red wine until dawn, then nap, then color champagne
with orange juice just so I can call it breakfast.

Sometimes I have nightmares. She comes in the form of a redhead.
She has a black mouth, no lungs. Fog spills from her lips.
When I'm awake, her name is *Mother.*

This is a picture of my scars.
I'm proving to you that they are mine.

Here, look closer:

Once, I knocked a neighbor girl onto the dirt and kicked her face because she
was walking through my yard and it was *my* yard.

Once, I closed my cat's tail in the door and I cried for days.

Once, I screwed up and I admitted it and it hurt and they shunned me anyway.

Once, I was jumped by a pack of skinheads.

Once, I loved.

Once, I loved.

Once, when I couldn't stop the wind, I broke the chimes.

ACKNOWLEDGEMENTS

With gratitude to the publications in which earlier versions of the following poems first appeared:

Danse Macabre: "beautiful: a legend," "the collection," "the lamb," "the witches," "Yellowfeather"

decomP: "plum"

FRiGG: "cleave," "mother, if in a museum," "the telling"

The Legendary: "40 love letters," "mama's girl," "numerology"

Lung: "cutters"

Naugatuck River Review: "The Great Hush"

The New York Quarterly: "presumption"

Not A Muse: The Inner Lives of Women, a World Poetry Anthology: "racing hummingbirds"

The November 3ʳᵈ Club: "Cross the Sea, Esman."

PANK: "communion," "exit wound," "unsolicited advice to adolescent girls with crooked teeth and pink hair"

Ragazine: "and/or," "untruth"

Spoken Word Almanac Project 2008 Anthology: "God replies.," "resurrection"

Further gratitude to the online publications where audio recordings of the following poems were originally released:

IndieFeed: Performance Poetry: "communion," "resurrection," "unsolicited advice to adolescent girls with crooked teeth and pink hair"

Ragazine: "and/or," "untruth"

ABOUT THE AUTHOR

JEANANN VERLEE is a former punk rocker who collects tattoos and winks at boys. Her work has appeared in a number of journals and anthologies, including *The New York Quarterly, FRiGG, PANK*, and *Not A Muse.* An acclaimed performance poet who co-curates the weekly reading series Urbana Poetry Slam at the Bowery Poetry Club, Verlee has performed and facilitated workshops across North America. She was coauthor and performing member of national touring company *The Vortex: Conflict, Power, and Choice!*, charter member of the annual *Spoken Word Almanac Project*, and is an ardent animal rights and humanitarian activist. She lives in New York City with her best pal (a rescue pup named Callisto) and a pair of origami lovebirds. She believes in you.

OTHER GREAT WRITE BLOODY BOOKS

EVERYTHING IS EVERYTHING (2010)
New poems by Cristin O'Keefe Aptowicz

DEAR FUTURE BOYFRIEND (2010)
A Write Bloody reissue of Cristin O'Keefe Aptowicz's first book of poetry

HOT TEEN SLUT (2010)
A Write Bloody reissue of Cristin O'Keefe Aptowicz's second book of poetry about her time writing for porn

WORKING CLASS REPRESENT (2010)
A Write Bloody reissue of Cristin O'Keefe Aptowicz's third book of poetry

OH, TERRIBLE YOUTH (2010)
A Write Bloody reissue of Cristin O'Keefe Aptowicz's fourth book of poetry about her terrible youth

THE BONES BELOW (2010)
New poems by Sierra DeMulder

CEREMONY FOR THE CHOKING GHOST (2010)
New poems by Karen Finneyfrock

MILES OF HALLELUJAH (2010)
New poems by Rob "Ratpack Slim" Sturma

YOU BELONG EVERYWHERE (2010)
Road memoir and how-to guide for travelling artists

LEARN AND BURN (2010)
Anthology of poems for the classroom. Edited by Tim Stafford and Derrick Brown.

STEVE ABEE, GREAT BALLS OF FLOWERS (2009)
New poems by Steve Abee

SCANDALABRA (2009)
New poetry compilation by Derrick Brown

DON'T SMELL THE FLOSS (2009)
New Short Fiction Pieces By Matty Byloos

THE LAST TIME AS WE ARE (2009)
New poems by Taylor Mali

Edited by Derrick Brown

LETTING MYSELF GO (2007)
Bizarre god comedy & wild prose by Buzzy Enniss

LIVE FOR A LIVING (2007)
New poems by Buddy Wakefield

SOLOMON SPARROWS ELECTRIC WHALE REVIVAL (2007)
Poetry compilation by Buddy Wakefield, Anis Mojgani, Derrick Brown, Dan
Leamen & Mike McGee

I LOVE YOU IS BACK (2006)
Poetry compilation (2004-2006) by Derrick Brown

BORN IN THE YEAR OF THE BUTTERFLY KNIFE (2004)
Poetry anthology, 1994-2004 by Derrick Brown

SOME THEY CAN'T CONTAIN (2004)
Classic poetry compilation by Buddy Wakefield

WWW.WRITEBLOODY.COM

WRITEBLOODY
QUALITY AMERICAN BOOKS

PULL YOUR BOOKS UP BY THEIR BOOTSTRAPS

Write Bloody Publishing distributes and promotes great books of fiction, poetry and art every year. We are an independent press dedicated to quality literature and book design, with an office in Long Beach, CA.

Our employees are authors and artists so we call ourselves a family. Our design team comes from all over America: modern painters, photographers and rock album designers create book covers we're proud to be judged by.

We publish and promote 8-12 tour-savvy authors per year. We are grass-roots, D.I.Y., bootstrap believers. Pull up a good book and join the family. Support independent authors, artists and presses.

Visit us online:
writebloody.com

CPSIA information can be obtained at www.ICGtesting.com
Printed in the USA
BVOW07s1212080914

365440BV00002B/21/P